# Sticker Dressing
# Heroes

Illustrated by Emi Ordás
Written by Megan Cullis
Designed by Lisa Verrall,
Emily Beevers & Lauren Ellis

## Contents

You will find all the stickers in the middle of the book.

Experts: Stuart Atkinson, Aaron Buckley (UN Mine Action Service), Patrick Conn, Pam Hickin (Cave Rescue Organisation), Dominic Hilton, Jim McMeekin, Sean Moore, Andy Pickard, Stuart Thompson and Steen Young

# Mountain rescue

At the bottom of a steep slope there's been a skiing accident, and an air ambulance has flown in to help.

A doctor and a medical worker, known as a paramedic, have just treated the injured skier's wounds. They wear reflective strips on their uniforms to make themselves visible in the snow. The pilot wears a radio headset to help him navigate the helicopter and communicate with the rest of the team.

Doctor

Paramedic

Pilot

# Lifeguards

On a busy beach, a swimmer has been swept out to sea. He's in serious danger, but an inflatable lifeboat is on its way. The lifeguards who patrol the beach are preparing to help too.

The jetski rescue lifeguard puts on a crash helmet to protect his head as he speeds through the water. Another lifeguard grabs a first-aid kit in case the swimmer is injured. They all wear bright red and yellow uniforms that show up clearly.

Jetski rescue lifeguard

First-aid lifeguard

Lifeguard in wetsuit

# Arctic explorers

Planet Earth is under threat. Temperatures are rising, causing sea ice in the Arctic to melt. These explorers are braving freezing temperatures, to try to find out why this is happening, and what to do about it.

An expedition scientist is using a drill to collect samples of ice to take back to the research base. Two explorers are preparing to collect some data. One of them wears a rubber suit to protect him from the freezing water, in case he falls through thin ice.

Expedition scientist

Explorer in a rubber suit

Explorer with skis

# Secret agents

Two secret agents are in hot pursuit of a gang of thieves, who have stolen some highly confidential government papers.

Agent Walker has been monitoring the thieves' movements and has tracked them down. Agent Stevens is gathering evidence with his camera, which is disguised as a briefcase. Police officer Cooper is ready to arrest the thieves. He wears a bulletproof vest in case they are armed.

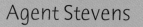

Agent Stevens

Police officer Cooper

Agent Walker

# Police diver

By a murky river, a team of police divers is investigating a murder. They're looking for a weapon buried in the riverbed. The water is polluted, so they wear drysuits to protect their skin, and face masks to help them breathe underwater.

# Coastal rescue

Far out at sea, a boat has capsized in a storm. The coastal rescue team has arrived to rescue the sailors from drowning.
This rescue officer is about to throw a lifebuoy into the water to keep them afloat. He's wearing a lifejacket and a safety helmet, in case he's thrown into the sea by the crashing waves.

Rescue officer

# Explosives expert

This explosives expert is searching for buried explosives, called land mines, which were laid in the ground during a recent war. It's very dangerous work because the mines could go off at any time. He uses a metal detector that beeps if there's a mine nearby. His dog can help sniff them out too.

# Mountain rescue pages 2-3

Follow the numbers and arrows to add the stickers in the right order.

① Doctor's boots

② Fire resistant waterproof flight suit

③ Latex gloves

④ Safety helmet

Safety helmet with visor and microphone ③

Fire resistant waterproof flight suit ②

Paramedic's boots ①

Pilot's boots ①

Fire resistant waterproof flight suit ②

Radio set to communicate with ground control ③

Helmet ④

# Lifeguards pages 4-5

Follow the numbers and arrows to add the stickers in the right order.

① Jetski lifeguard's trunks

Safety helmet ③

First-aid lifeguard's shoes ①

Shirt and lifejacket ②

Trunks ②

Shirt and binoculars and belt bag ④

High visibility swimming cap ③

Sunglasses ③

Cap ②

Lifeguard's trunks ①

# Arctic explorers pages 6-7

Follow the numbers and arrows to add the stickers in the right order.

Polar bear

Explorer's rubber immersion suit ①

⑥ Clipboard for recording measurements

① Explorer with skis' insulated ski boots

② Wind-proof ski pants

⑤ Insulated jacket

④ Wind-proof ski pants

③ Insulated jacket with furry hood

③ Insulated hiking boots

Thick gloves ④

⑤ Ski poles

② Thick gloves

⑥ Skis

① Expedition scientist's wool hat

# Secret agents pages 8-9

Follow the numbers and arrows to add the stickers in the right order.

Running shoes
③

Baseball cap
④

② Jeans and gun in holster

① Police officer Cooper's shirt and bulletproof vest

⑤ Handcuffs

Stray cat

① Agent Stevens' shoes

Pigeon

④ Camera disguised as a briefcase

Black jeans
②

③ Shirt and trench coat

⑤ Sunglasses

Strong boots
④

Tough gloves
②

Leather motorcycle jacket
③

⑤ Sunglasses

Motorcycle helmet
⑥

① Agent Walker's motorcycle leathers

# Police diver page 10

Follow the numbers and arrows to add the stickers in the right order.

③ Hood, oxygen mask and light

② Waterproof gloves

④ Rubber fins

Police diver's drysuit and air cylinders ①

Dive panel to monitor the diver's air supply

# Coastal rescue page 11

Follow the numbers and arrows to add the stickers in the right order.

Rescue officer's waterproof gloves ①

Boots ②

⑦ Safety helmet

⑥ Lifebuoy

③ Thick waterproof drysuit

Lifejacket ④

⑤ Rope

# Explosives expert page 12

Follow the numbers and arrows to add the stickers in the right order.

Metal detector ④

⑤ Blastproof padded apron to protect against explosions

Thick overalls ③

② Tough full face visor

① Blastproof boots

# Astronaut page 13

Follow the numbers and arrows to add the stickers in the right order.

② Soft leg protection

Rigid body protection, life support system and 'bubble' helmet ③

④ Protective gloves

① Astronaut's boots

⑤ Wrench

# Paratroopers

Follow the numbers and arrows to add the stickers in the right order.

① Pathfinder's gloves

Camouflage pants ②

Camouflage helmet ④

Camouflage jacket and reserve parachute ②

③ Boots

Camouflage jacket and breathing equipment ③

Wrist compass ④

① Officer's camouflage pants

Soldier's camouflage pants ①

② Camouflage jacket and chest pack for equipment

⑤ Boots

③ Boots

④ Rifle

⑤ Helmet

Parachute

⑥ Helmet and oxygen mask

Equipment and supplies

# Cave rescue pages 16-17

Follow the numbers and arrows to add the stickers in the right order.

Drill to put bolts in the cave wall for help with climbing

Rescue worker's gloves ①

① Rescue diver's wetsuit hood

② Rubber gloves for warmth and protection

Wetsuit with depth gauge attached to chest ③

④ Helmet with light attached

② Waterproof oversuit made of tough fabric

Rubber boots ③

Rubber boots ③

④ Harness

② Thick PVC oversuit with harness

Warm air reviver

④ Helmet with light attached

⑤ Helmet with lights attached

Tackle bag containing caving equipment

⑦ Wetsuit boots

⑥ Compact mask

Underground controller's gloves ①

Follow the numbers and arrows to add the stickers in the right order.

Fireproof hood ②

Fireproof jacket ③

① Fire stuntman's fireproof leggings

④ Gloves

⑤ Boots

Camera operator

Face mask ⑤

Director

Flexible, stretchy suit with markers ②

Stretchy hood with markers ③

① Superhero's shirt with bulging chest muscles

Gloves ④

Sidekick's durable gloves with markers ①

Lightweight shoes with markers ④

Shoes ③

② Leggings

# Firefighters pages 20-21

Follow the numbers and arrows to add the stickers in the right order.

① Firefighter's boots

Chemical spills firefighter's gloves ①

Chemical containers

Thick rubber suit containing breathing equipment ②

② Fireproof pants

Helmet ⑥

Fireproof tunic and light ⑤

④ Hatchet for getting into buildings

③ Gloves

Firefighter's metalized pants and boots ①

Rubber boots ③

② Metalized jacket and gloves

Protective hood containing breathing equipment ③

# Earthquake rescue
## pages 22-23

Follow the numbers and arrows to add the stickers in the right order.

① Team leader's overalls

② Boots

⑤ Gloves

Helmet and breathing mask

③ Equipment belt

④ Hand-held radio

⑥ Gloves ④

⑤ Carbon dioxide detector

① Team specialist's helmet

② High visibility overalls

③ Boots

# Bomb disposal expert page 24

Follow the numbers and arrows to add the stickers in the right order.

⑥ X-ray machine to examine unexploded bombs

⑤ Neck protector plate

④ Bomb-proof jacket and breast plate

② Covered boots

① Bomb expert's pants

③ Helmet with visor

# Astronaut

On the International Space Station – a research station that circles the Earth in space – an astronaut is making an emergency repair. He wears a spacesuit with a life-support system on his back. This keeps him alive in space where there's no air to breathe.

Astronaut

# Paratroopers

Paratroopers are landing in a dangerous war zone, close to enemy lines. They're soldiers, trained in parachuting, who jump from planes and helicopters into areas that are difficult to reach by land.

   The pathfinder jumps first – his job is to mark out the area where the other soldiers can land. The officer who commands the group is ready to go into battle. He and the other soldier wear face paint to camouflage their skin.

Officer                                                    Soldier

Pathfinder

# Cave rescue

Deep inside a cave, an explorer is being rescued after a violent fall of rocks dragged him into the water. A cave rescue team is working quickly to get him out.

Wearing lights on his helmet and a wetsuit, the rescue diver has just pulled the injured explorer out of the pool. In his tackle bag, he carries a harness to lift him out of the cave. An underground controller, who oversees the operation, is ready to help the other cave explorers out of the cave.

Rescue diver

Underground controller

Rescue worker

# Stuntmen

These fearless stuntmen are performing on the set of a superhero movie. The fire stuntman wears a heatproof suit. A performer on wires is about to do some superhero flips in the air. The superhero's sidekick wears a suit covered in markers. This allows computers to turn his movements into an animation in the finished movie.

Fire stuntman

Superhero

Superhero's sidekick

# Firefighters

A huge explosion has ripped through a factory, setting oil storage tanks on fire. A firefighter in a metalized suit is ready to tackle the flames. Another firefighter, in a rubber suit, is there to clear some dangerous chemical spills. Breathing equipment inside the suit stops him from breathing in the poisonous fumes.

Firefighter

Firefighter in metalized suit

Chemical spills firefighter

# Earthquake rescue

A huge earthquake has destroyed lots of buildings. Within minutes, a search and rescue team arrives, ready to help anyone who has been trapped or injured.

They carry equipment to listen for sounds underneath the rubble, in case there are people trapped down there. A search and rescue dog is trained to search areas that are difficult for humans to reach.

Search and rescue team leader

Search and rescue dog

Team specialist

# Bomb disposal expert

A bomb has been planted on a train. This bomb disposal
expert is operating a robot, which can stop the bomb
from exploding. In case of accidents, he's wearing a
full bodysuit, heavily plated on the inside.

Bomb disposal expert

First published in 2012 by Usborne Publishing Ltd., 83-85 Saffron Hill, London, EC1N 8RT, England.
www.usborne.com Copyright © 2012 Usborne Publishing Ltd. The name Usborne and the devices ♀ ⊕ are
Trade Marks of Usborne Publishing Ltd. All rights reserved. No part of this publication may be reproduced, stored in a
retrieval system, or transmitted in any form or by any means, electronic, mechanical, photocopying, recording or otherwise,
without prior permission of the publisher. Printed in Perai, Penang, Malaysia. First published in America in 2012. A.E.